TABLE OF CONTENTS

INTRODUCTION

It's your favorite bulldog of all time—don't tell
the oters!—Ronny, here. Are you ready for a new adventure?

Last time, we embarked on a journey all over the world,
discovering all sorts of neat, interesting facts. For those of you
that weren't with us for that wondrous adventure, allow me to
introduce myself: I'm Ronny. I used to be an ordinary bulldog,
enjoying belly rubs and doggie treats all day, every day. I lived in
Paris, where I'd go for daily walks around the Eiffel Tower.

One day, I decided to change things up and climbed to the top of
the tower. You have to do that at least once, you know. The only
problem is, I climbed the tower in the middle of a thunderstorm.

It was very cool and windy up there, but very dangerous too.

 **Then, BOOM!** 

I got struck between the eyes with a bolt of lightning. Can anyone say bullseye? The lightning bolt changed me, kind of like how a radioactive spider bite can change you. My brain grew immensely in size, and I suddenly became incredibly intelligent. My brain began to crave knowledge and information, the same way my belly craves bananas—believe me, it craves a LOT of bananas. They're my favorite food.

Anyway, my hunger for knowledge only increased as time passed. So, I packed up all my stuff and all my bananas and took off to see the world. I discovered all sorts of fascinating things about science, history, and even languages.

During my travels, I came across an incredible place called China. You know, where the massive Chinese Wall is. The place that invented fireworks and dumplings, which are quite tasty, even if they aren't bananas. I could only stay a really short time in China but now, at last, it's time to go back. It's time to discover one of the most fascinating things that China has to offer. No, it's not dragons, though those are pretty cool, too. It's the Chinese language.

QUICK FACT:

Did you know that about 1.4 billion people speak Chinese as their main language? Outside of China, Chinese is spoken in countries like Malaysia, Indonesia, and Singapore!

What's so fascinating about the Chinese language?

Well, you see, Chinese isn't really like any other language in the world. They do not have an alphabet, after all! That's right. Instead, China has characters. These are shapes that represent words and ideas by using visual elements and pictures. The word for "person", for example, looks like a standing man, and the word for "sun" looks like the sun with its rays around it.

(Evolution of the character person - 人)

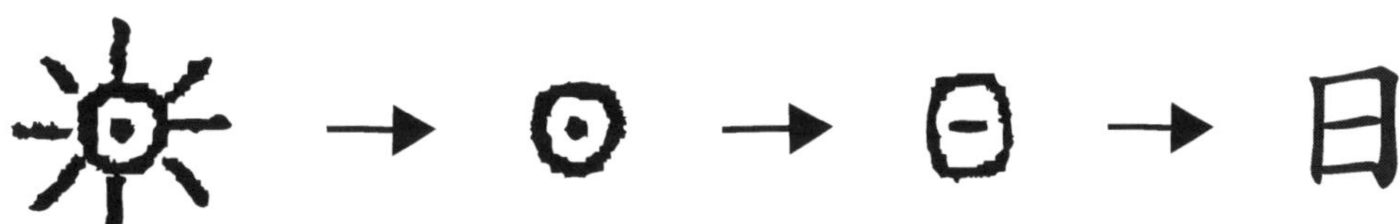

(Evolution of the character sun - 日)

The Chinese language can be as difficult as it is cool, though.

This is because there are as many characters as there are words! Can you imagine memorizing all of those characters? Sounds impossible, right? Well, luckily you don't have to know every single character in the world. You can learn the most essential ones and then turn things into a game. How many more characters can you learn?

Wait, why are there so many characters in the first place?

Why didn't the Chinese just come up with a regular, old alphabet, instead of this challenging game? This is all thanks to a man called Cangjie, who was asked to do so by the Yellow Emperor. The emperor of China was known as the Yellow Emperor because he glowed like the sun. He told Cangjie to come up with some sort of written language for his country.

The four-eyed Cangjie—yes, he had four eyes!—studied the sun, moon, and stars.

Thanks to his great eyesight, he was able to find special characters that fit each of these things. When he was done, the Chinese gods wept because they feared Cangjie's invention would make the Chinese people smarter and more cunning!

All of this happened thousand of years ago, of course.

The Chinese language is so old that the first characters were written on turtle shells and animal bones because paper hadn't been invented yet!

Later, people started writing them on bronze plaques, and then on paper. By then, the characters had changed and evolved quite a bit, with more being added to them every day. Some still looked like the physical things they represented. Others didn't. Today, Chinese characters use a lot of straight lines, which makes them easier to read and learn.

Are you ready to learn, then?

Are you ready to venture into China and discover all the cool characters that are out there? Are you ready to expand on your knowledge and feed your brain with me, after we've had a snack break, of course?

CHAPTER 1:
FAMILY WORDS

Family is one of the most important things in the world. You have a nightmare, you go to your mommy. You had a fight with a friend, you talk to your daddy. You want advice, you go to your brother or sister. You want a belly rub and—wait, I think that's just me.

Family is especially important in most Asian cultures. There's this thing here called xiao in Chinese, which means filial piety. It's the idea that you must always value, be loyal to, love, respect, and obey your parents and elders. You can practice xiao by doing things like

- listening to your parents and grandparents carefully and following their guidance

- expressing your love, gratitude, and appreciation to your family both through words like "please" and "thank you".

爸爸

bàba

Dad

妈妈

māma
Mom

姐姐

jiějie
Older sister

姐					

哥哥

gēgē
Older brother

弟弟

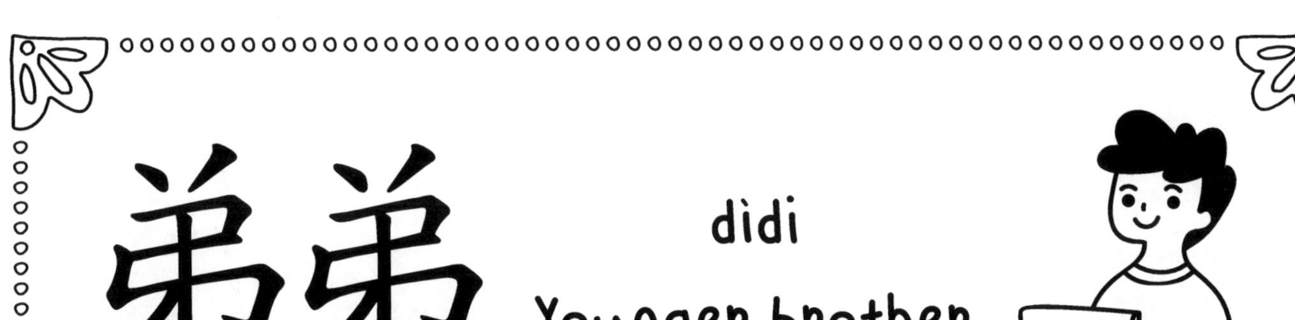

didi

Younger brother

妹妹

15

爷爷

yéye

Grandpa

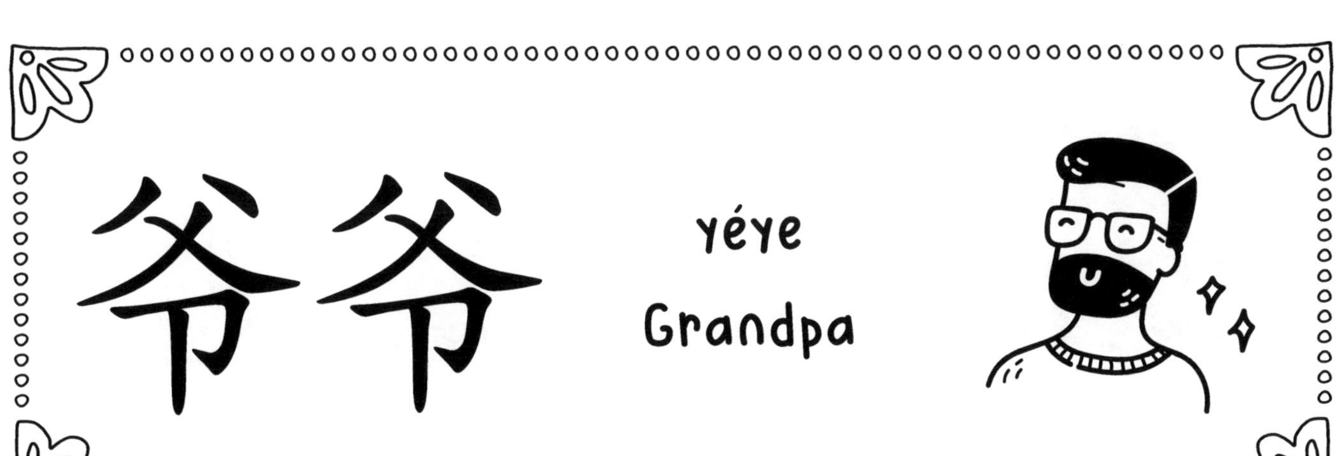

奶奶

叔叔

shūshu

Uncle

阿姨

āyí
Aunt

CHAPTER 2: DESCRIBING NATURE

THERE'S NOTHING QUITE LIKE BEING OUTDOORS AND IN NATURE.

A good picnic in the shade of some trees, feeling the wind on your face, playing fetch… Nature is important to us all, but it plays an immense role in Chinese philosophy. This philosophy divides nature into five elements that fit together like puzzle pieces: Metal, wood, fire, water, and earth. These five elements have very special relationships with each other. They help each other to grow through mutual generation and restraint. As an example, water helps wood grow by giving plants the water they need. This is "generation". Fire, meanwhile, controls metal by melting it. That's "restraint".

金

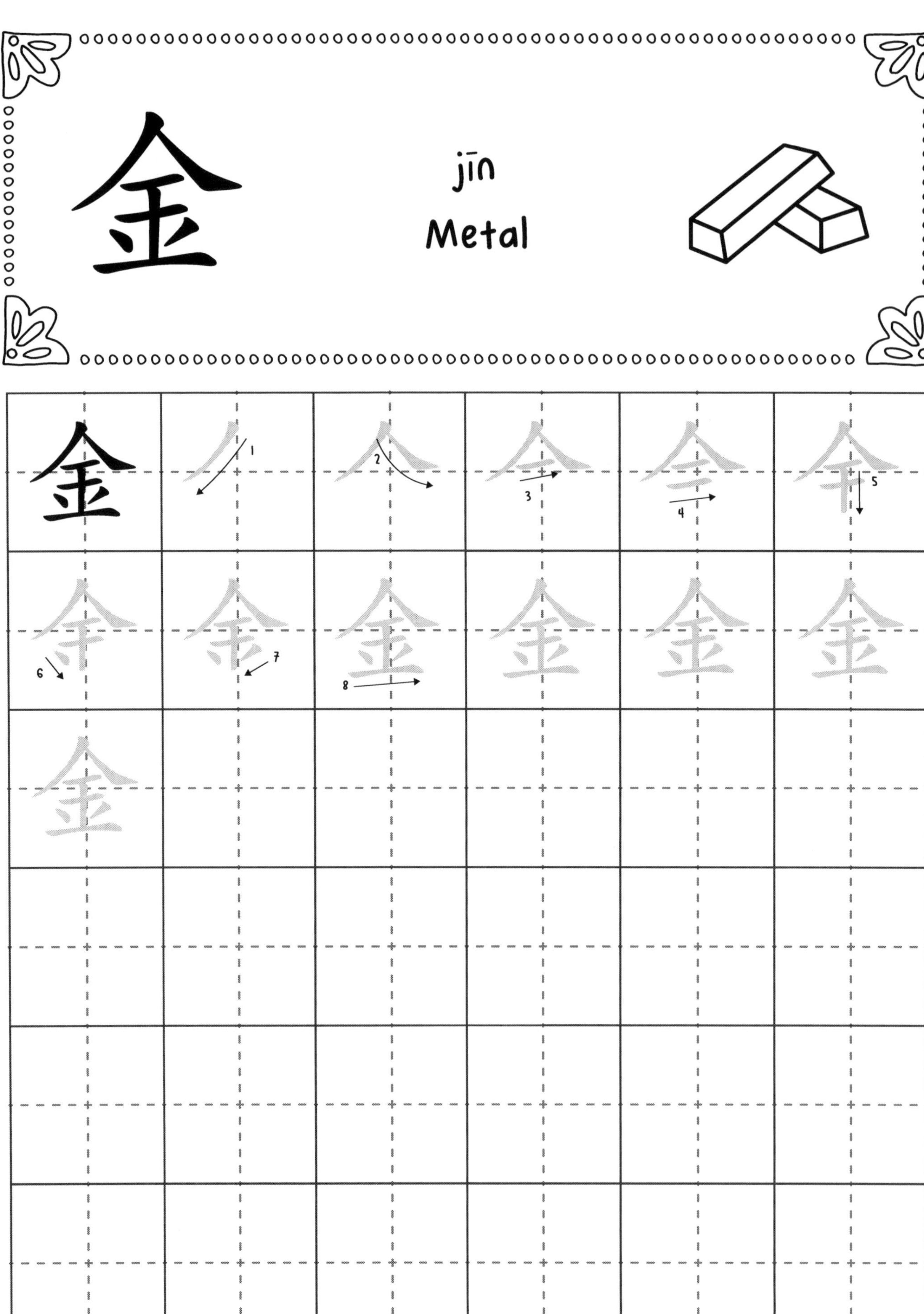

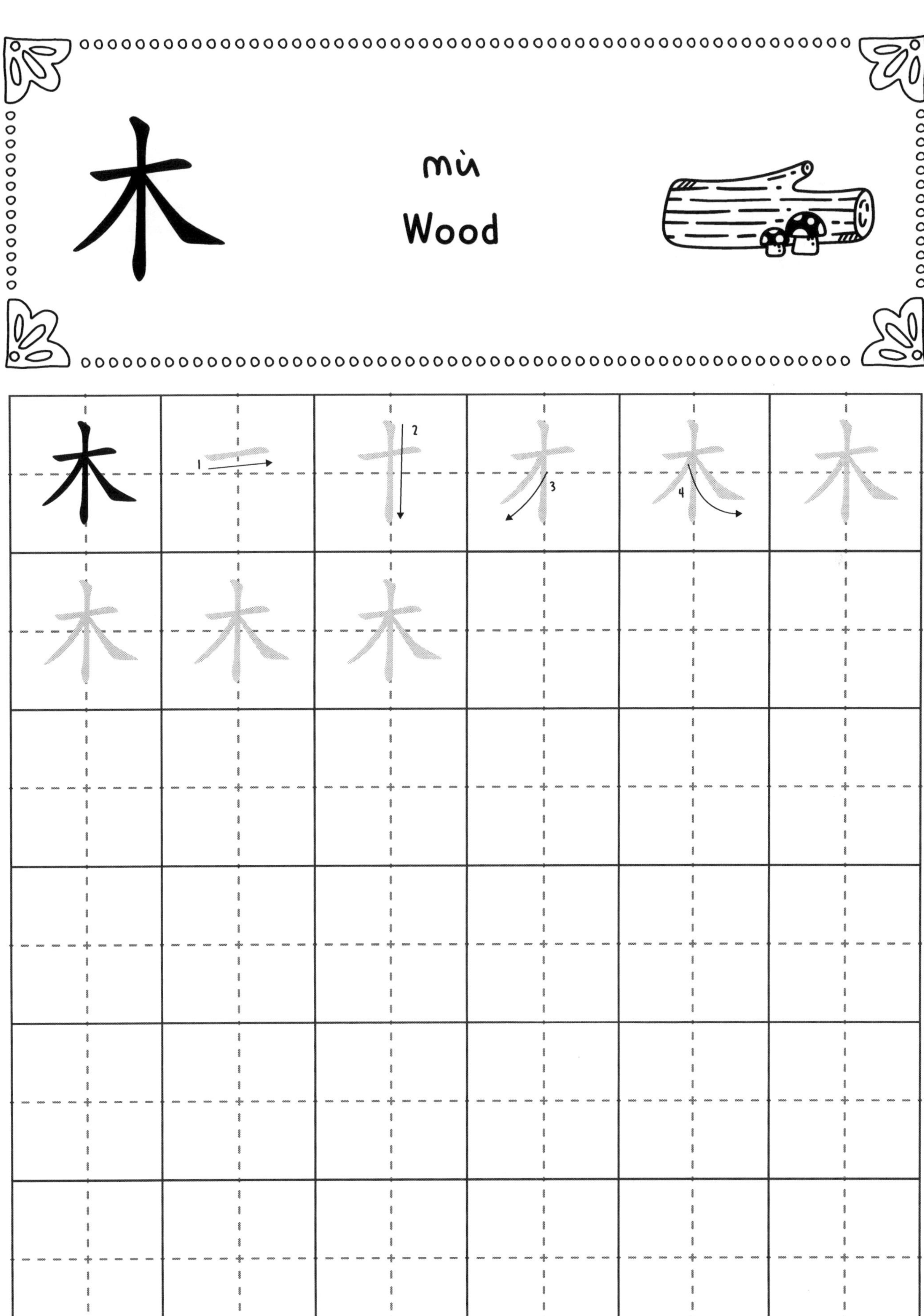

mù
Wood
木
一
十
才
木
木
木
木
木

水

shuǐ

Water

火

huǒ

Fire

土

tǔ
Earth

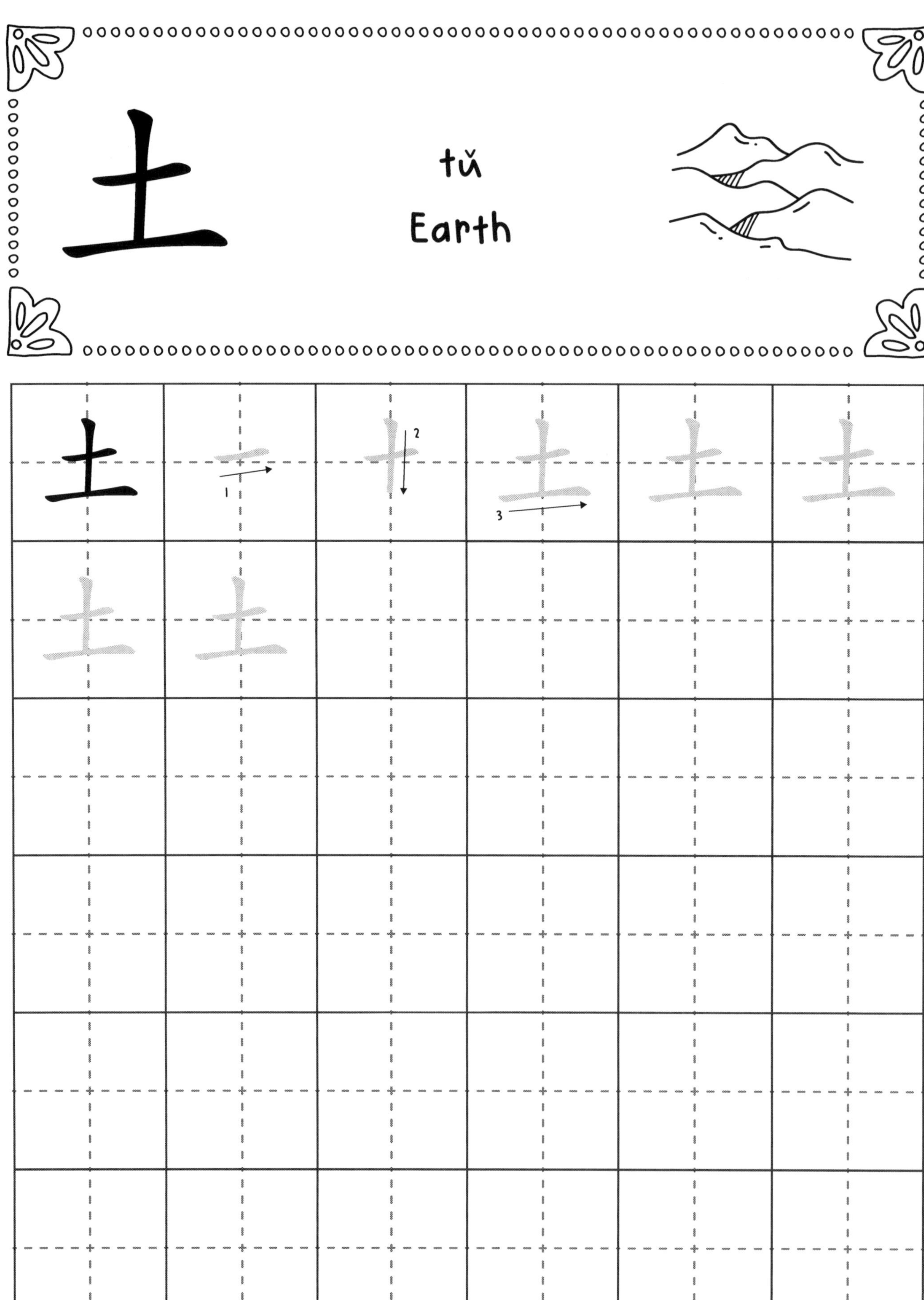

山

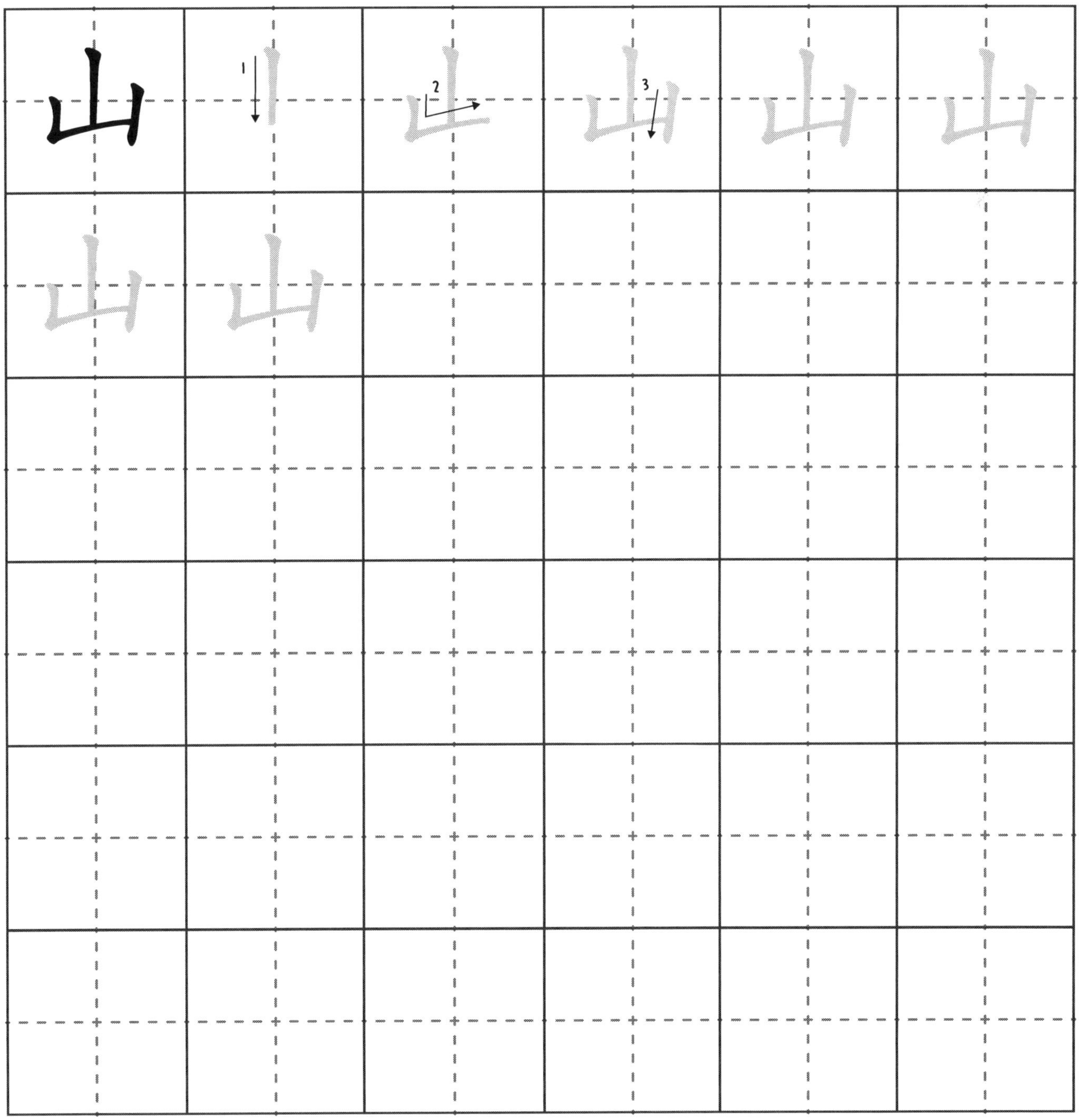

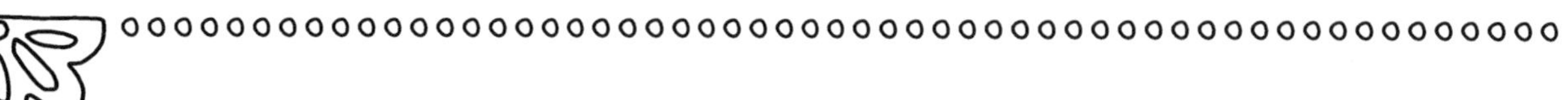

花

树

shù

Tree

天空

tiān kōng

Sky

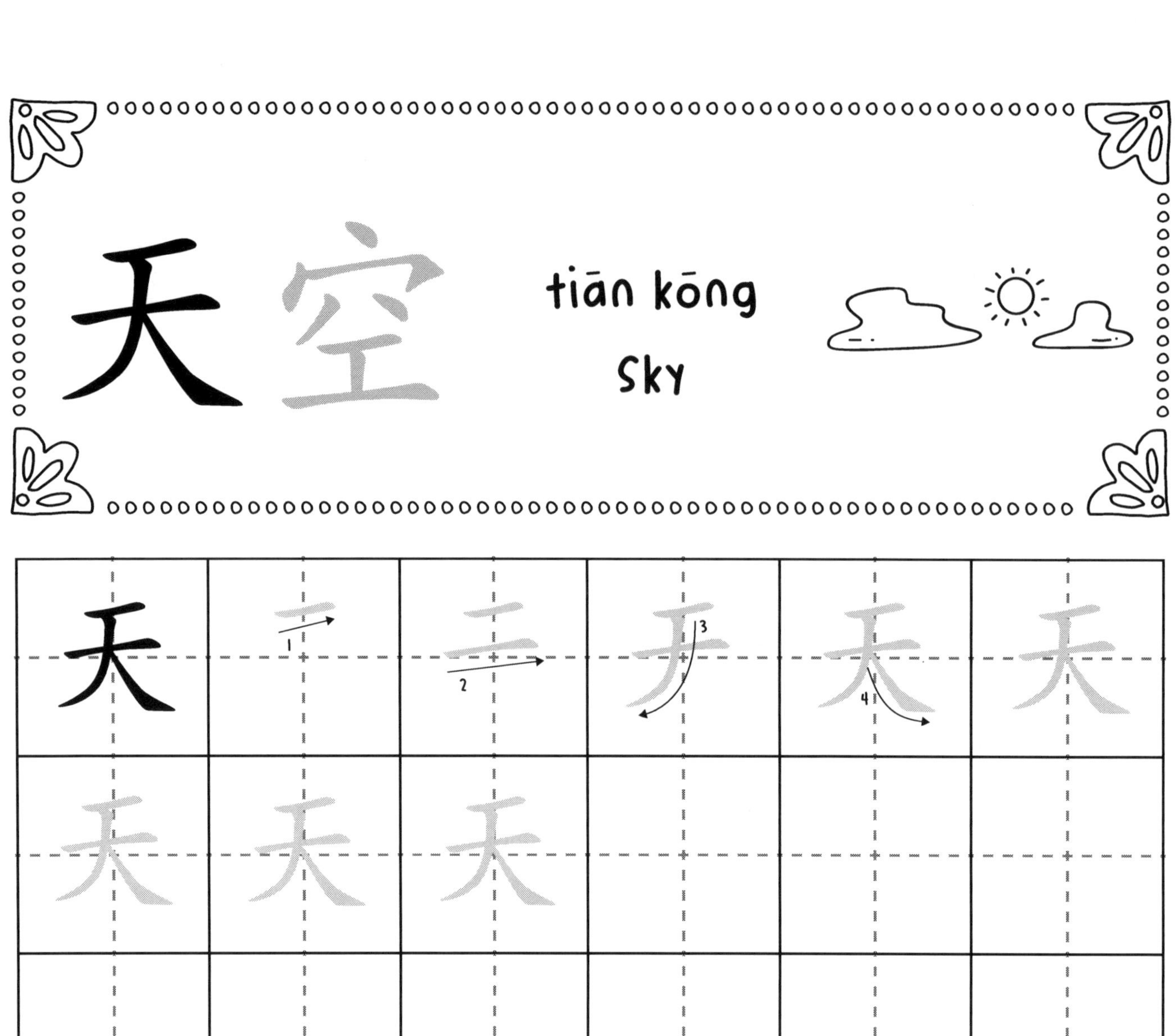

天空

tiān kōng

Sky

鸟

niǎo

Bird

雨

太阳
tài yáng
Sun
太
一
大
太
33

太阳

tài yáng

Sun

云

yún

Cloud

月亮

yuè liàng

Moon

月亮

yuè liàng

Moon

星星

xīng xing

Stars

大海

大海

dà hǎi
Ocean

海

湖

hú
lake

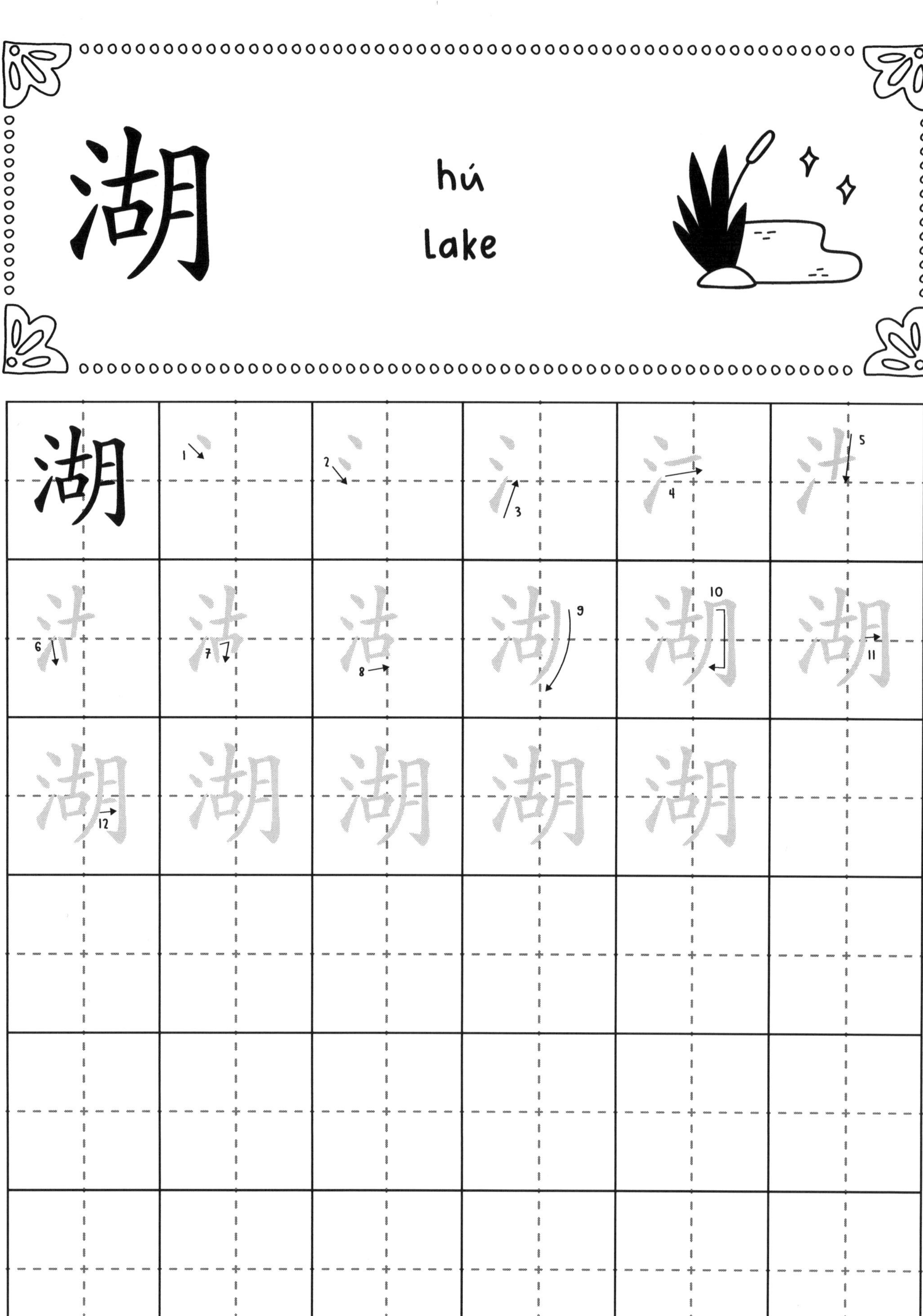

雪
xuě
snow

CHAPTER 3:
HOW ABOUT SOME FOOD?

YOU ALREADY KNOW WHAT MY FAVORITE FOOD IS, SO WHAT'S YOURS?

Here's a better question: What's your favorite Chinese food? I think mine might be dumplings. Perhaps yours are noodles? Have you ever tried dim-sum before? If you haven't, I'd recommend it! Dim-sum is a kind of Chinese cooking that originated in Southern China and that's made up of lots of bite-sized dishes like dumplings. They're served in bamboo baskets and, by the time you're done, you feel absolutely stuffed! How about fortune cookies? I'm sure you've tried some. Do you remember what your fortune was? Did you know that fortune cookies aren't actually a Chinese custom? No, they were invented in San Francisco, of all places, in 1914, by a Japanese worker called Makoto Hagiwara.

米饭

mǐfàn

Rice

米饭

mǐfàn

Rice

面条

miàntiáo
Noodles

46

面条

miàntiáo

Noodles

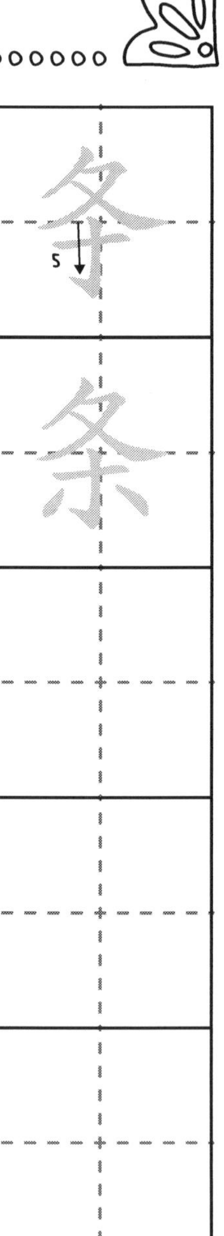

包子

bāozi

Steamed bun

包

饺子

jiǎozi
Dumpling

水果

蔬菜

shūcài

Vegetables

蛋

jīdàn

Egg

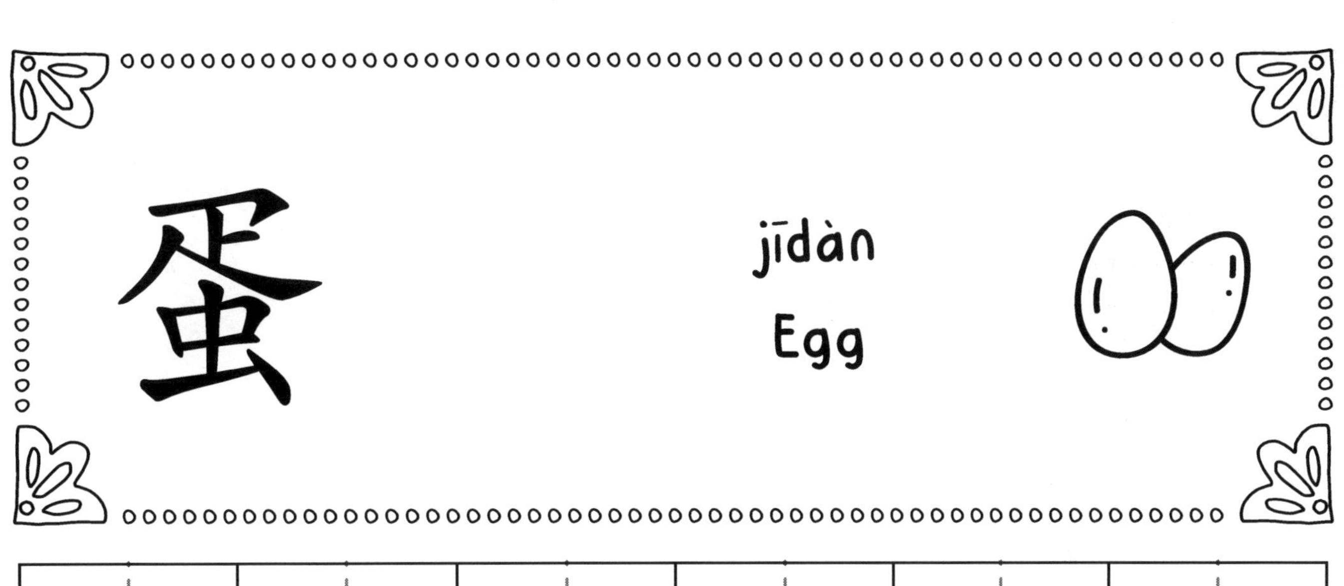

糖

táng
Sugar, Candy

茶

chá

Tea

CHAPTER 4: YOUR BODY PARTS

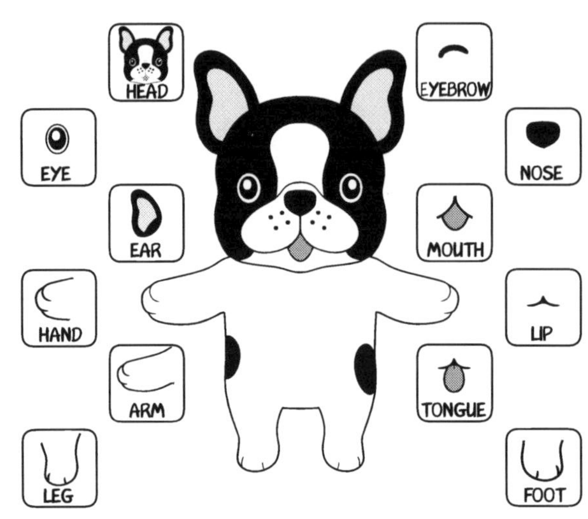

REMEMBER HOW NATURE WAS A BIG PUZZLE IN CHINESE PHILOSOPHY?

Well, the human body is too, at least in Chinese medicine. Each body part, like your mouth, lungs, and hands, is connected to one another. The connections between them run on invisible lines of energy called meridians. Because of these meridians, when one part of the body, like your liver, is healthy and happy, other parts of your body are too. When there's something wrong with a body part, though, there are suddenly problems with other parts of your body. This is why you need to take care of every part of your body. Your mouth, for example, is connected to your stomach. So, you have to chew your food well for your stomach to be able to digest it well.

DOES THAT MAKE SENSE?

眼

鼻子

bízi
Nose

口
kǒu
Mouth

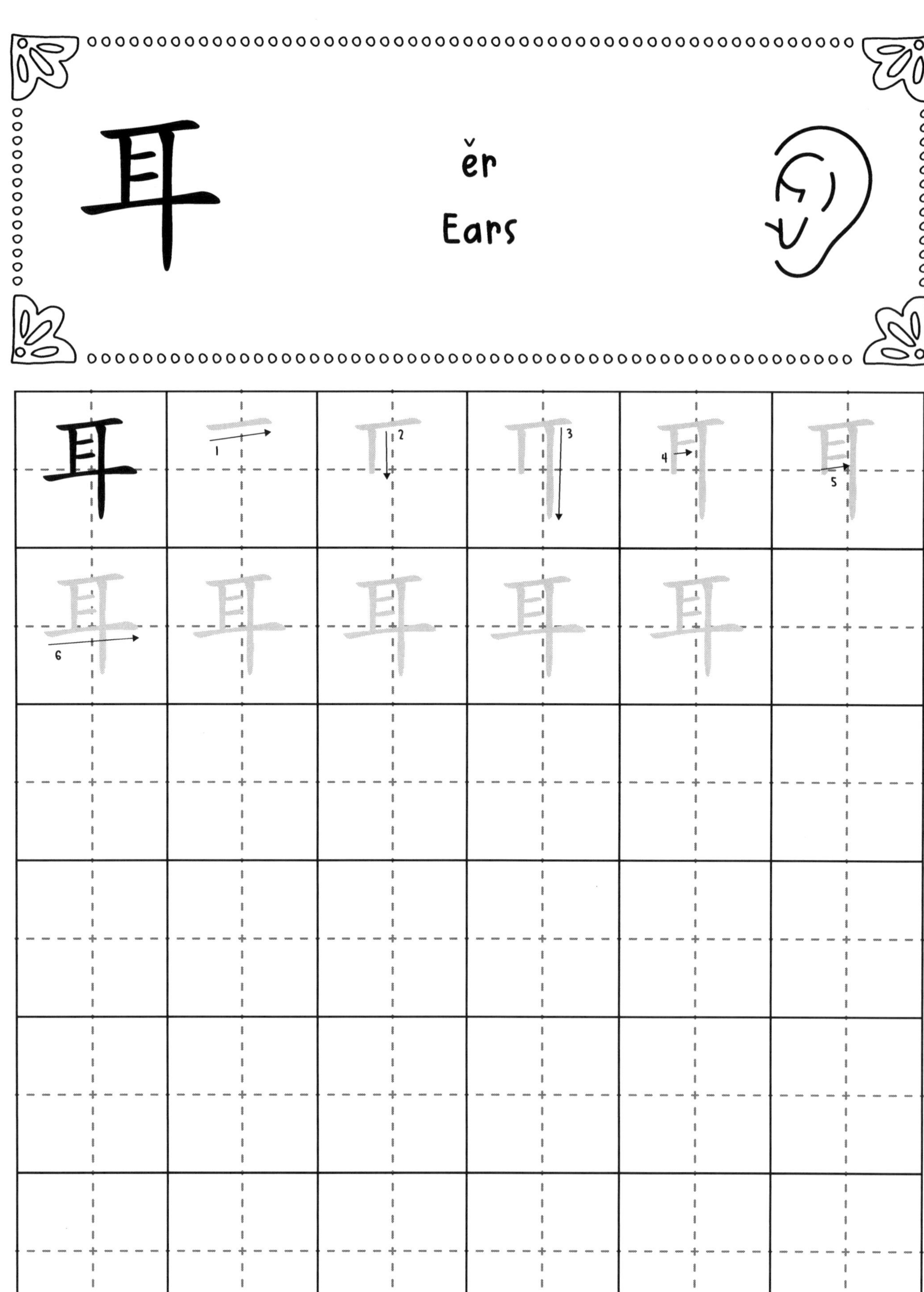

耳

ěr

Ears

头发

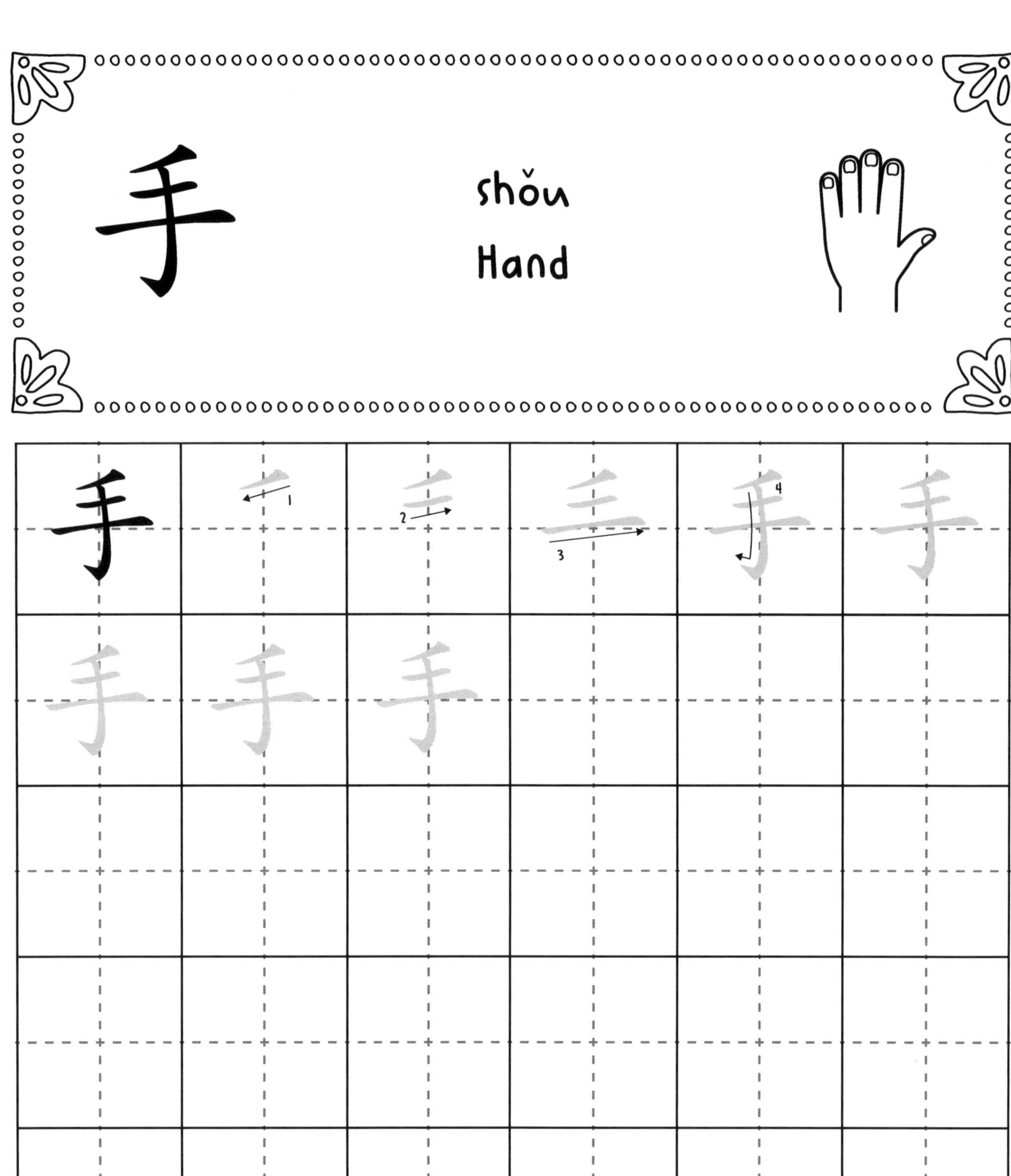

手

shǒu

Hand

脚
jiǎo
Foot

肚子

dùzi

Stomach

腿

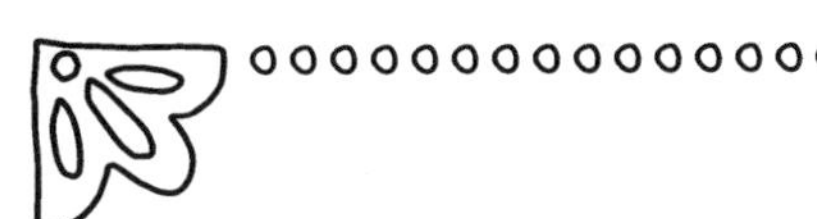

脸

liǎn

Face

CHAPTER 5: EVERYDAY LIFE

HOW DO YOU LIKE SPENDING YOUR DAY?

I usually take a wash after waking up. Then, I decide which collar I want to wear and speak—well, bark at—my parents to give me food. After eating, we'll play together a bit. My favorite games are fetch, and "hide your owner's left shoe before they go to work". After that, I choose a good book and read for a bit. Sometimes, I find some pen and paper and write or draw instead. Then, I study my Chinese characters. It's night by the time I'm done, so I go to sleep after that! Here's a fun idea:

WOULD YOU LIKE TO TRY DESCRIBING YOUR DAY USING CHINESE CHARACTERS?

书

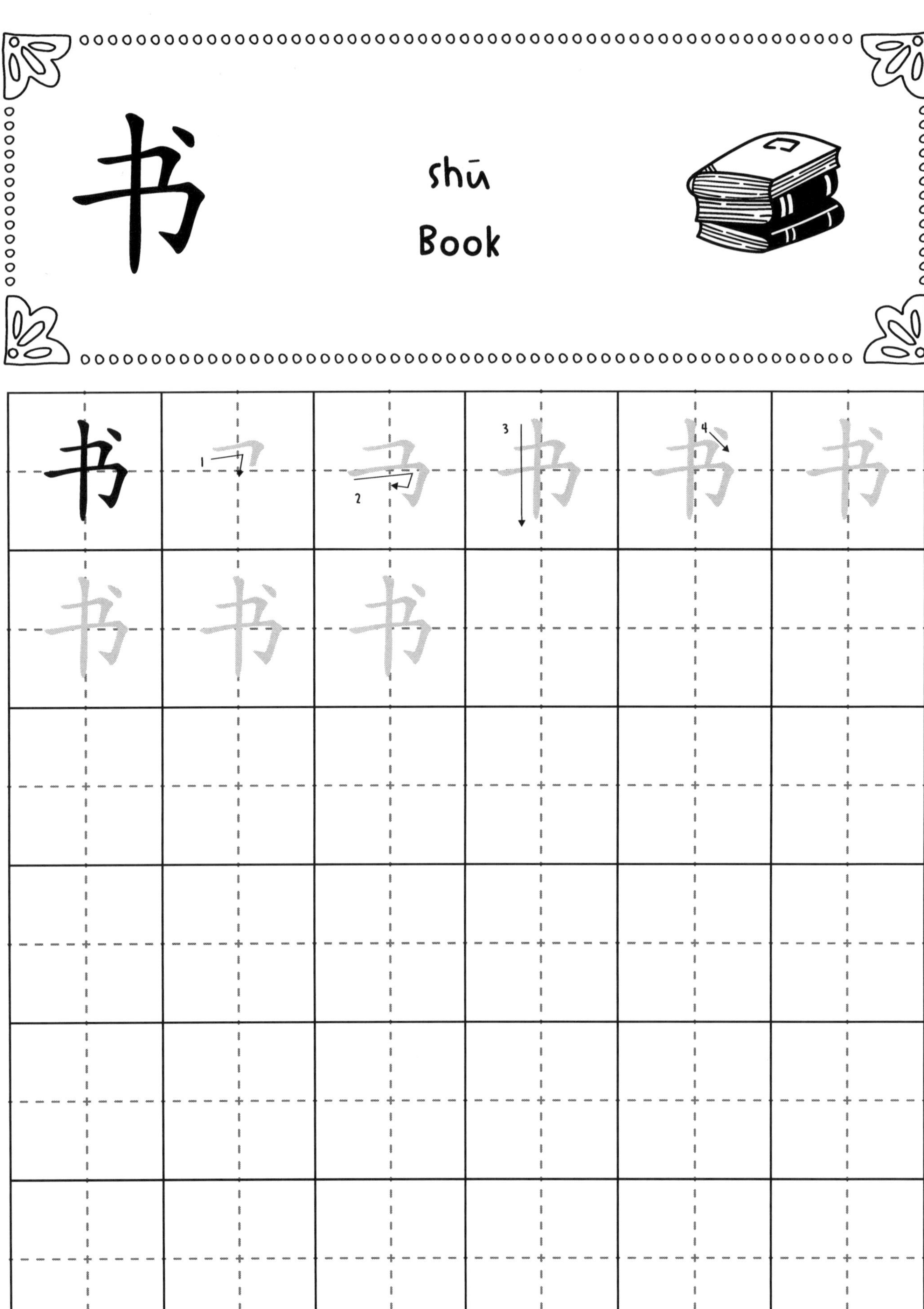

笔

bǐ

Pen

纸

学

xué

Study

吃

chī

Eat

睡

shui

Sleep

玩

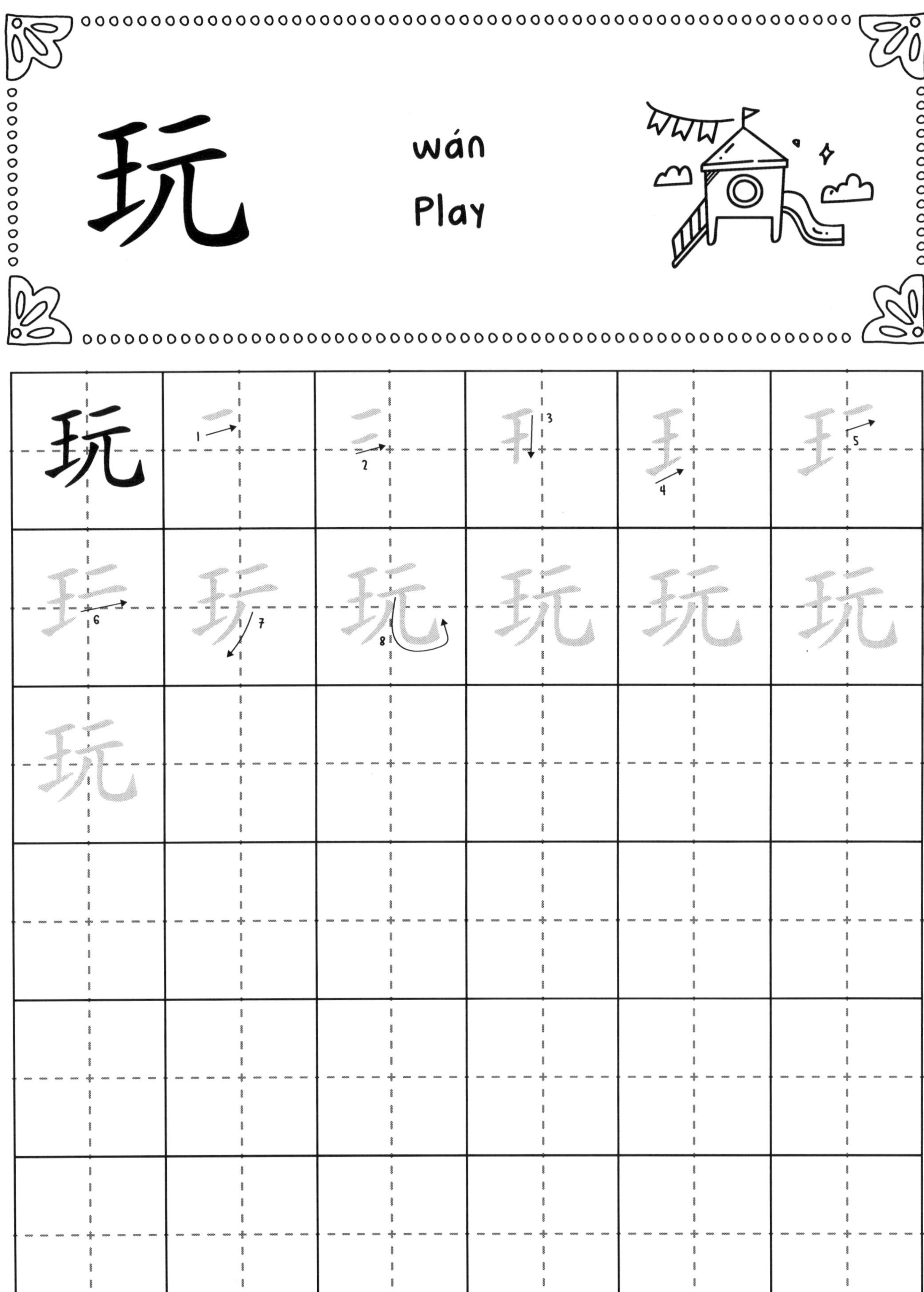

看

kàn
Read/Watch

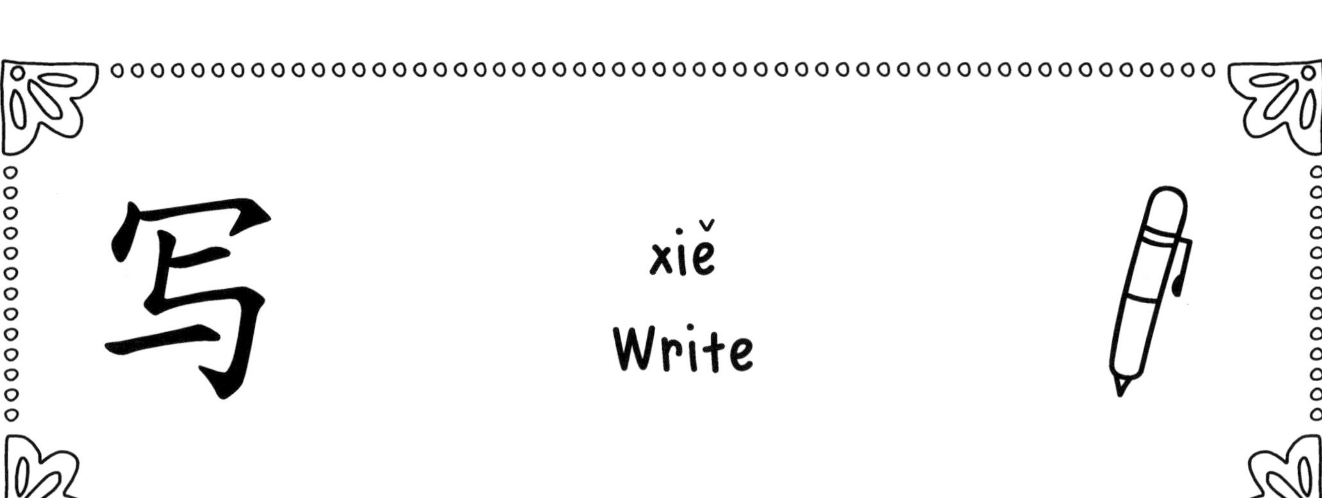
写
xiě
Write

画

洗

xǐ

Wash

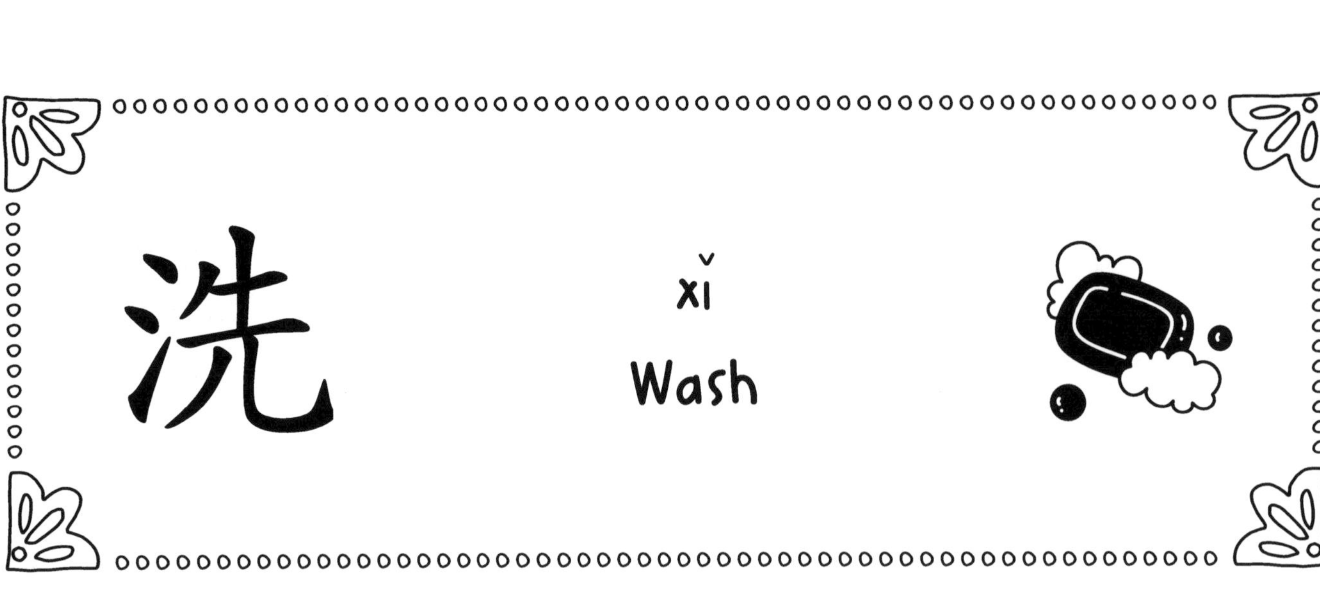

穿

chuān

Wear

说

shuō

Speak

CHAPTER 6: STAYING AT HOME

GOING OUT WITH FRIENDS AND ON WALKS IS REALLY FUN, BUT SOMETIMES YOU JUST WANT TO STAY HOME AND RELAX.

Home is a special place, somewhere you always feel safe and comfortable, somewhere that's always harmonious and peaceful. In Chinese culture, it's the foundation of the family, which is very important, as you know. That's why the Chinese character for home (家) actually represents a roof over a pig!

HOW FUNNY IS THAT?

家

jiā

Home

门

mén
Door

窗

chuāng

Window

床

chuáng

Bed

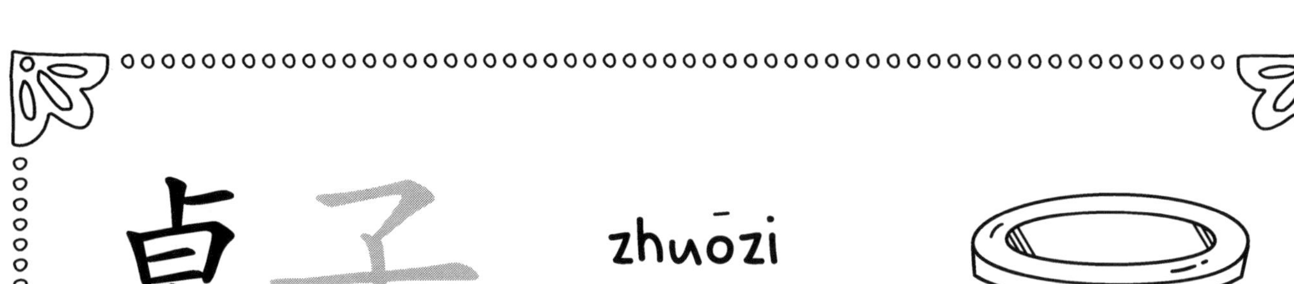

桌子

zhuōzi

Table

椅子

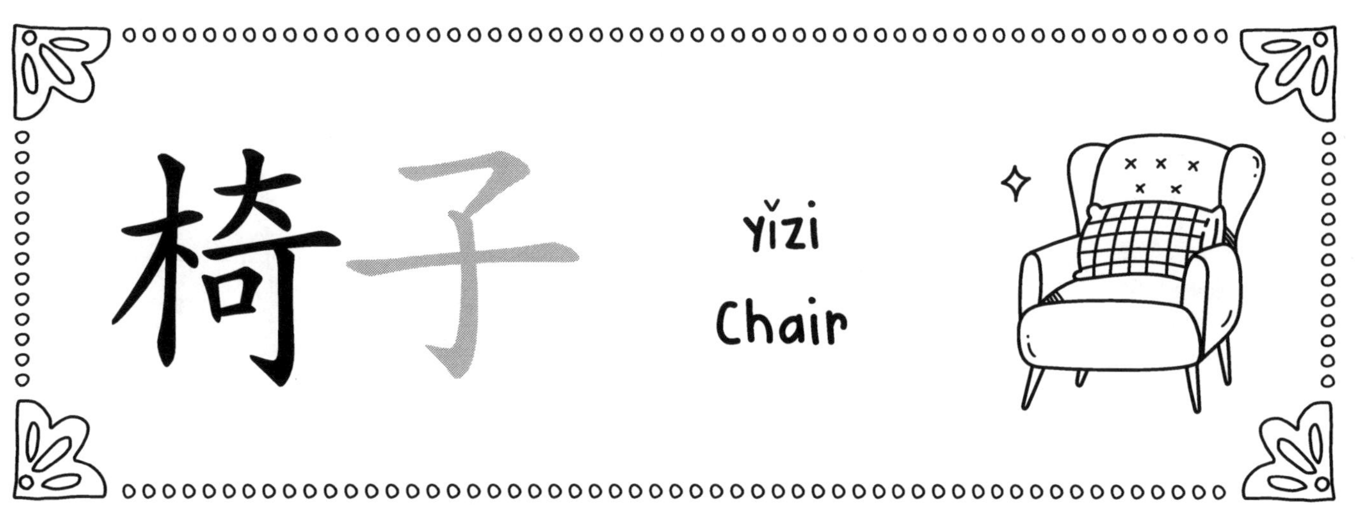

电视

diànshi
Television

diànshi
Television

灯

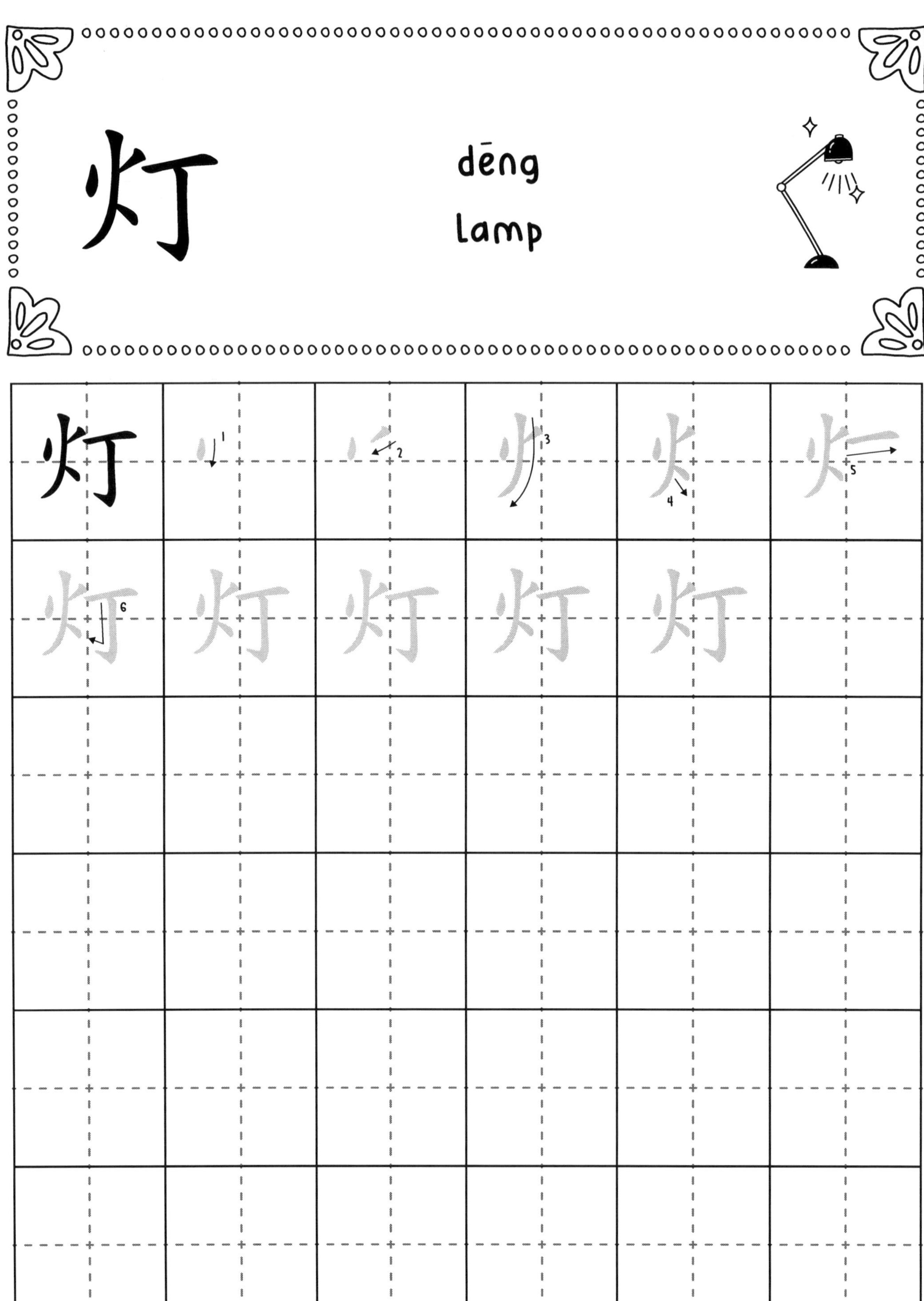

柜子

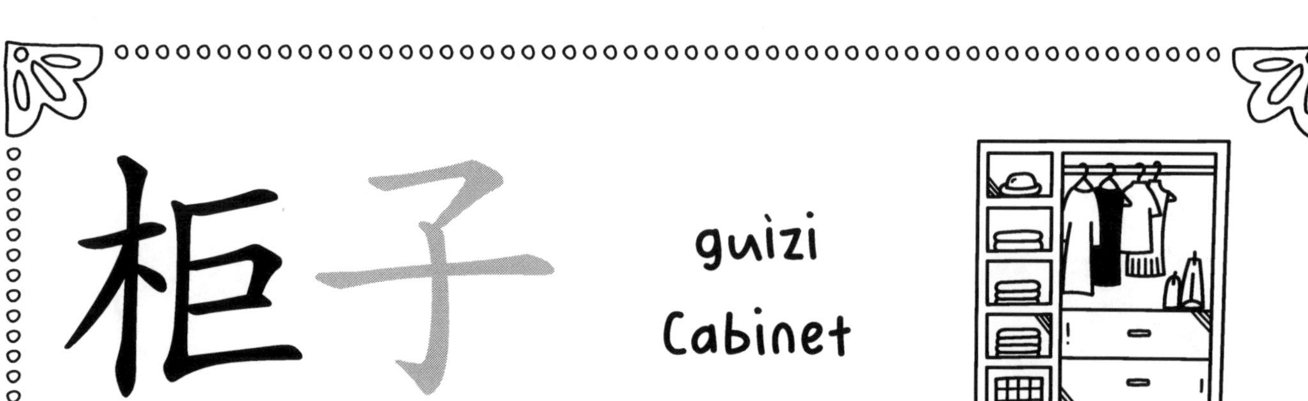

镜子

CHAPTER 7: YOUR EMOTIONS

YOUR EMOTIONS ARE THINGS THAT HELP YOU TO EXPRESS HOW YOU FEEL.

If someone throws you a surprise birthday party with a great cake, you'd feel happy. If a good friend was moving from France, where you live, to China, you'd be sad. You'd be excited to visit them in Beijing, the capital of China, though! You can communicate all these emotions and more to the people around you, so long as you know the words for them.

开心

kāixīn

Happy

开心
kāixīn
Happy

难过

nánguò

Sad

难

1 2 3 4 5 6 7 8 9 10

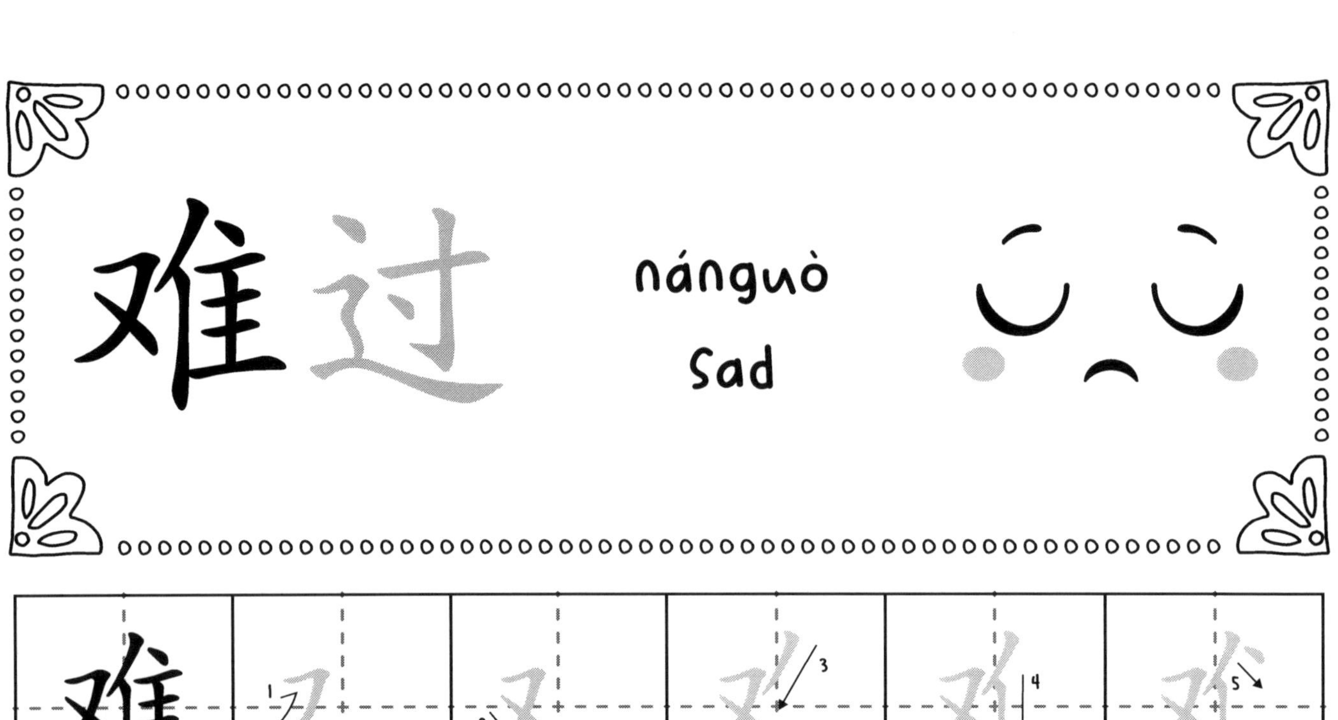

难过
nánguò
Sad

生气

shēngqì
Angry

生气
shēngqì
Angry

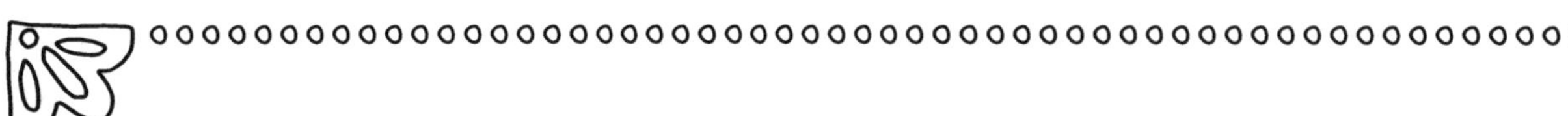

兴奋

xīngfèn

Excited

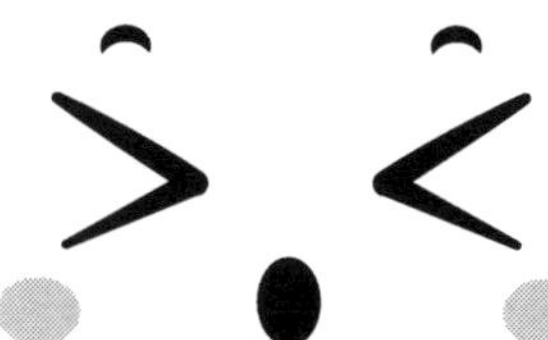

兴奋

xīngfèn

Excited

害怕

hàipà

Scared

害怕
hàipà
Scared

爱

CHAPTER 8:
THE CHINESE ZODIAC

WHAT'S YOUR ZODIAC SIGN?

There are 12 zodiacs in Chinese culture. Each zodiac corresponds to a year and is associated with a specific animal. People born in the year of that animal get its unique traits. Did you know that the rat is the first zodiac in the calendar?

You see, years ago, the Jade emperor, who was the divine ruler of all things, organized a race among all animals. The rat wasn't the fastest animal, but he was the most cunning. So, he went to the ox and convinced him to carry him on his back across the river. As they neared the shore, he leaped off of the ox's back and raced ahead. So, the rat ended up getting first place and the honest, hardworking ox got second place. If I had been around for this race, though, I would have ended up winning first place and becoming the first zodiac!

鼠

shǔ

Rat

牛

niú

Ox

虎

hǔ
Tiger

兔

tù

Rabbit

龙

lóng
Dragon

蛇

马

mǎ

Horse

羊

yáng

Sheep

猴

114

狗

gǒu

Dog

猪

zhū

Pig

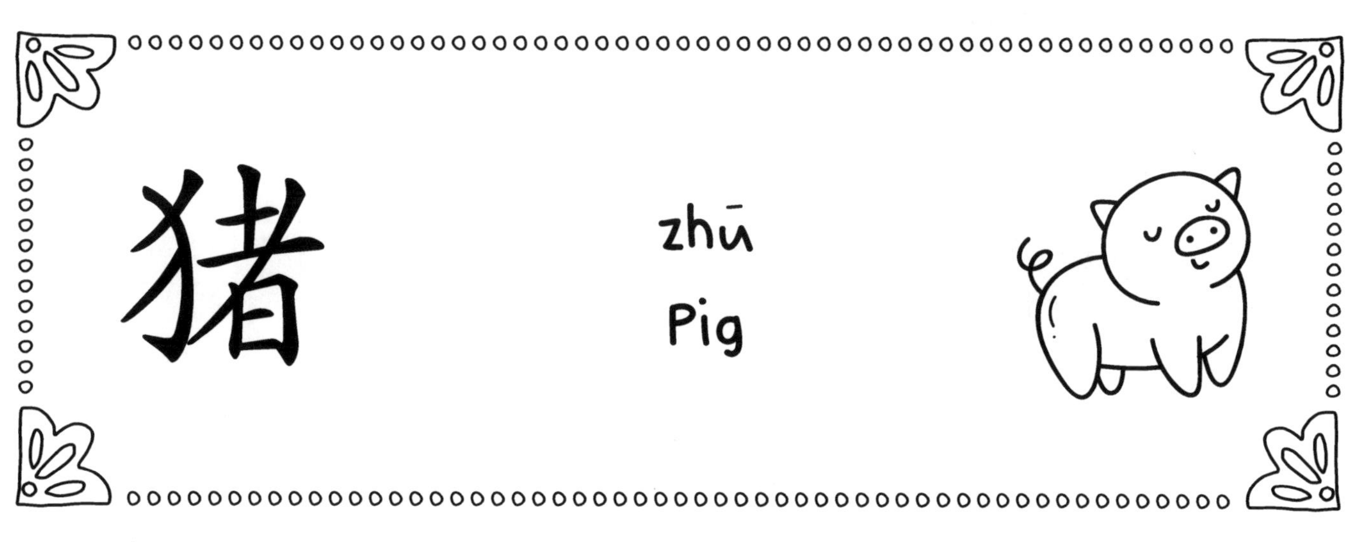

CONCLUSION

Here we are, at the end of another grand adventure with Ronny the Frenchie.

I can't believe how many different things we learned! That was so much fun, wasn't it? I hope you enjoyed exploring the world of Chinese characters as much as I did. I don't know about you, but now I'm going to go ahead and put what I've learned to good use. Time to roll up my sleeves, adjust my collar, and practice the new characters that I have learned. I wonder how many I'll be able to memorize and perfect.

My goal is to get as many as I can as perfectly as I can! After that, perhaps I'll go ahead and learn some more new characters.

What about you?

Would you like to join me as I learn even more characters and practice the ones that we learned together?

Here's an idea:

Would you like to hold a little competition to see who can memorize and perfect their Chinese calligraphy more quickly? If you do, let's quickly pull out our notebooks. Pens at the ready and…

Ready, set, go!

All done with your practice? That's great. You beat me to it! In that case, I look forward to our next practice session, and perhaps we'll meet on another adventure soon.

Take care till then and keep practicing!

Thanks for coming along on another journey with me and learning about the Chinese characters. I think you did a great job!

Join me once again and dive into the captivating stories of extraordinary sport heroes and fearless entrepreneurs. I can't wait to share their remarkable tales of innovation and determination with you. In addition to the inspiring stories, I have included some fantastic coloring pages that will spark your creativity too!

So, what are you waiting for? Claim the freebies by scanning the QR code below or type riccagarden.com/ronny_freebies into your web browser.

(Note: You must be 16 years or older to sign up, so grab your parent for help if you need to.)

Your Frenchie,
RONNY

Made in the USA
Middletown, DE
05 December 2024